The
CUILLINS

Carlton

DIAL
PRESS

First published 1994

ISBN 0 7110 2292 5

© Ray Carlton 1994

Published by Dial Press

an imprint of Ian Allan Ltd,
Terminal House, Station Approach,
Shepperton, Surrey TW17 8AS.
Printed by Ian Allan Printing Ltd,
Coombelands House, Addlestone,
Weybridge, Surrey KT15 1HY.

Contents

65
Previous page:
**Ghreadaidh, Mhadaidh
and Bidean seen from
Loch Coruisk**

58
Right:
**The Misty Isle hides the
secrets of the Cuillins**

9
Far right:
**A climber views the Sron
na Ciche precipices from
the Cioch**

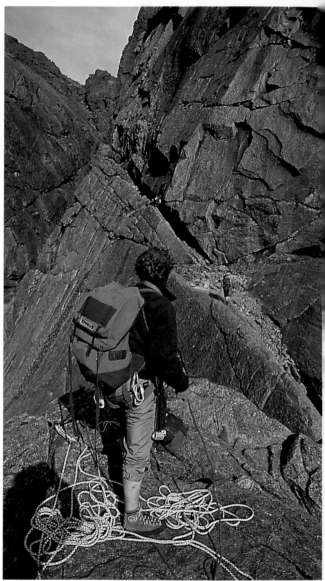

Introduction

The Cuillins! To anyone who has visited and climbed these majestic mountains the mere mention of the name conjures up visions of precipitous rock faces, tottering pinnacles, airy peaks and mysterious corries.

The Cuillin Hills were 'discovered' in the 1800s and quickly became a climbers paradise. Few of the peaks had ever been reached before, and the last summit to be climbed — Sgurr Coir nan Lochain — was not ascended until 1896. The whole of the Main Ridge traverse was not completed in one day until 1911, when Shadbolt and MacLaren attempted this gruelling feat. The 'Greater Traverse', including Blaven and Clach Glas had to wait until 1939, when Charleston and Forde completed the task. Four of the summits are named after their conquerors, a unique honour in the British Isles — Alasdair after Sherrif Alasdair Nicholson, Thearlaich after Charles Pilkington, Thormaid after Norman Collie and Mhic Coinnich after John Mackenzie.

Today, the peaks are climbed more often than ever before, with increasing numbers of visitors discovering the delights of climbing on the rough Cuillin gabbro, a heavy crystalline volcanic rock which gives superb grip, wet or dry, on modern Vibram boot soles but is very hard on the skin. The summits remain essentially unchanged — the Main Ridge links 23 peaks, with 11 tops being greater than the 3,000ft altitude required for 'Munro' status, named after Sir Hugh Munro who attempted to climb and catalogue all the high peaks in Scotland.

I first visited the Cuillins in 1979 but didn't succeed in reaching the Main Ridge until my second visit in 1980, when I climbed to the top of Sgurr Alasdair via the Great Stone Chute — a truly memorable experience. From that moment I have regarded these mountains with reverence, and in six subsequent visits I have climbed to most, but not all, of their summits. I have found the scenery to be without equal in the British Isles and, apart from the lack of glaciers, the rock formations along the Main Ridge are very reminiscent of the tottering ridges of the high Alps.

In this Photographic Guide the traverse of the Main Ridge is divided into five sections, each of which can be tackled comfortably in a day's climbing, with a return back to the starting point on foot. The degree of difficulty on the routes ranges from simple but strenuous walking to roped rock climbing, although in most cases the difficult parts can be avoided by a detour, often by descending to a lower level before re-ascending to the ridge.

Section 1 covers the southern peaks of the Cuillin, from Gars Bheinn to Sgurr Dubh na da Bheinn. This section comprises mainly simple walking, although some scrambling towards the end necessitates the use of both hands and feet. Only the last two peaks, Sgurr nan Eag and Dubh na da Bheinn, reach a height of 3,000ft.

Section 2, from Sgurr Alasdair, the highest summit on Skye, to Sgurr Dearg covers one of the best known areas of the Cuillin. Progress here ranges from strenuous walking over scree to exposed scrambling, with no serious difficulties other than a descent at the western end of the Inaccessible Pinnacle for which a rope must be used.

Section 3, from Sgurr Dearg to Ghreadaidh is the longest section and takes in four 3,000ft summits, with the exposure on the traverse of Ghreadaidh being particularly hair raising.

Section 4, from Sgurr a' Mhadaidh to Bruach na Frithe, is the most technically difficult of all, with route finding around the tops and fissures of Mhadaidh, Bidean Druim nam Ramh and An Caisteal being especially tricky.

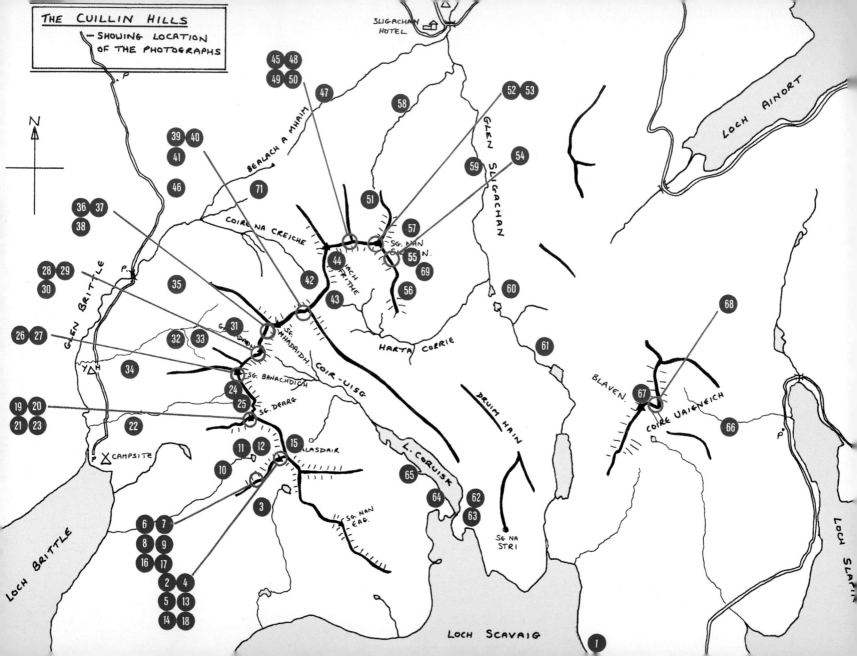

Section 5, the last section on the Main Ridge, extends from Sgurr a' Fionn Coire to na h-Uamha and includes the famed traverse of Sgurr nan Gillean.

Apart from the climbs on the Main Ridge, this guide also includes two further routes. The walk to Loch Coruisk, Section 6, although very long, should not be missed as this has some of the best panoramic scenery in Scotland. Finally, Section 7 describes the Blaven — Clach Glas traverse, a technically difficult scramble in some of the most impressive rock scenery on Skye.

Access to the Cuillins is quite difficult, since there are few roads close to the mountains and accommodation is limited in the immediate area. Sections 1 to 4 commence in Glenbrittle, where the Youth Hostel or the campsite can provide shelter from the vagaries of the weather on the Island. Sections 5 and 6 start from Sligachan, where the Hotel provides an excellent base, the accommodation and food being to a high standard. The new 'Seumas Bar-Restaurant', which serves hot food all day, is a recent and welcome addition to the historic hotel. There is also a campsite run by the Hotel. Section 7 can be reached after a drive from Broadford where there are several hotels and cafes.

No introduction to a book about the Cuillins would be complete without a few words of warning regarding the weather on the Misty Isle of Skye! Most of the photographs in this book show the peaks in glorious sunshine. This is, however, a moderately rare occurrence! Due to the moist sea air the Cuillin can be completely shrouded in mist when the rest of the island is basking in sunshine. Furthermore, the local weather conditions can change at the drop of a glove and a climber who sets out in fine weather can find himself having to navigate in less than 10m visibility without warning. The twists and turns of the Ridge render route-finding very hazardous in these conditions — especially so because the rocks are highly magnetic and compass errors of up to 90 degrees can be seen. A recent proliferation of new cairns on some of the more popular routes has compounded the difficulties. In my experience, under worsening conditions the safest way down from the ridge is to retrace one's steps unless the way ahead is very familiar, because what often appears to be an easy route down can turn into a precipice!

Notwithstanding these warnings, in good visibility and if care is taken, these climbs can provide days of supreme enjoyment and memories which last for many years to come. Slainte mhor!

21
Below: **The West ridge of Sgurr Dearg**

Right: **The Cuillin with Gars-Bheinn from Loch Scavaig**

At about 400m (1,300ft) above sea level one reaches a plateau with several small tarns. The route to Gars-Bheinn now leads straight up the smooth scree slope until the crest of the ridge is attained, with cliffs falling sheer into Coire a' Chruidh on the northern side. The ridge slants upwards and the crest is followed until the dry-stone walled shelter at the summit is reached. This is frequently fully occupied by climbers during the early part of the day, but in mist or rain, as it was when I was last there, one can expect to rest in splendid isolation before tackling the Main Ridge.

A well defined grassy track descends northwest from here towards Sgurr a Choire Bhig, the next summit on the ridge, which is attained after a short descent and re-ascent across two subsidiary tops.

The walk is short and exhilarating and from the summit at 875m (2,870ft) the long curving ridge to Sgurr nan Eag can be seen. This is a simple undulating walk of around 1 km distance (half a mile) but, due to the sheer nature of the cliffs on either side, the path should on no account be abandoned.

From a dip at 773m (2,535ft) the path turns first due west, then northwards and skirts some huge boulders until the summit of Sgurr nan Eag (924 m, 3,031ft) is reached. This 'Peak of the Cliff' is the first 'Munro' on the route.

Section 1 — Gars-Bheinn to Sgurr Dubh na da Bheinn.

This first section of the main Cuillin ridge begins with the most southerly peak — Gars Bheinn. At a height of 910m (2,984ft) it just fails to qualify as a 'Munro', but in its open situation its shapely half-conical form can be seen to advantage from Loch Scavaig and from Elgol. The southwestern side slopes steeply down to the sea in a continuous sweep, whilst sheer cliffs fall away on the north towards Loch Coruisk.

The summit of Gars-Bheinn is the normal starting point for the traverse of the whole of the main Cuillin ridge. It can either be reached from Loch Coruisk by skirting round the rocks of the southernmost promontory or, preferably, from Glenbrittle campsite by walking across the grass and heather for a distance of 5 km (3 miles). The route initially follows a well defined track and, after crossing the All't Coir a' Ghrunnda stream, a gently rising sheep track leads southwest. The low lying island of Soay is in view for most of this distance.

2

Left: **Gars-Bheinn to Sgurr nan Eag from Alasdair**

The ridge now turns northwards and is level but rocky for almost 0.5km before slanting down towards Coire a' Ghrunnda. The first real difficulty is now approached — Caisteal a' Garbh Coire, a huge block of the heavy and rough minerals Gabbro and Peridotite sits athwart the ridge. This obstacle can be overcome directly by a short rock climb but is easily turned on the west (Ghrunnda) side by a rocky traverse.

3

Below left: **Caisteal a' Garbh Coire and Sgurr nan Eag**

The ridge regained, the next peak Sgurr Dubh na da Bheinn (938m, 3,078ft) is ascended by a steep scramble up grooves and boulders, with a final steep section which can be turned on the left. From the summit, the twin peak of Sgurr Dubh Mor (944 m, 3,096ft), the reigning Munro, can be reached by a short detour to the East which involves a difficult scramble to the top. Sherrif Nicholson first reached the summit by this route in 1874.

4
Opposite: **The Dubhs from the Summit of Alasdair**

The Main Ridge continues northwest with a rough scramble over rock steps to the dip at Bealach Coire an Lochain. This is a good point to break off the traverse if the whole ridge is not being tackled in one day. The following ascent to Sgurr Thearlaich is blocked by the notorious and sensational 'Thearlaich-Dubh gap' which can only be passed by a 10m abseil into the gap, followed by a 25m climb up a slippery basalt chimney. This route is graded 'Very Difficult' and best left to the rock expert.

The gloomy Coire a' Ghrunnda can be reached by descending the scree to the northern end of the loch.

5
Left: **Coire a' Ghrunnda from the head of the Great Stone Chute**

6
Opposite: **The Sgumain Stone Shoot and the Ladies' Pinnacle**

It is best not to attempt to leave the corrie by the stream as huge smooth boiler-plate slabs, devoid of holds for boot or hand, bar the exit. Instead, the scree slopes to the west of Sgurr Sgumain should be ascended to the head of the Sgumain Stone Shoot, which is easily recognised (even in mist) by the Ladies' Pinnacle to the right.

From this point there is a magnificent view across Coire Lagan to the scree slopes of An Stac and the Inaccessible Pinnacle on Sgurr Dearg. If time and stamina permit, the rocks to the western side of the stone shoot should be climbed to the almost level top of Sron na Ciche.

7
Centre: **The Inaccessible Pinnacle and An Stac**

On following the rim of the cliffs, a cleft is reached from which the remarkable Cioch pinnacle can be viewed. This can be attained from above by a steep and exposed scramble, but the route up from the valley floor is a rock climb, graded 'Severe', of around 300m in height.

8
Left: **The Cioch from Sron na Ciche**

9
See Page 3:
A climber views the Sron na Ciche precipices from the Cioch

To descend back to Glenbrittle, the steep but easy Sgumain Stone Shoot should be followed down into Coire Lagan. The broad path across the peat to the campsite is joined on crossing the All't Coire Lagan stream.

10
Right: **The Sgumain Stone Shoot and the Cioch from the floor of the Corrie**

This section of the Cuillin takes in the Round of Coire Lagan — arguably the finest mountain climbing anywhere on Skye, or indeed anywhere in the British Isles. From the highest point, Sgurr Alasdair, all 20 peaks of the Cuillin ridge can be seen.

The route leaves Glenbrittle from the campsite and the wide well-tramped path across the peat is followed into Coire Lagan. At around 450m altitude, there is a steeper section where slabs are crossed to reach the upper corrie. The corrie presents a beautiful scene; 300m high encircling cliffs and scree slopes sweeping down to a still sheet of clear water, the tiny loch Lagan.

11
Left: **Coire Lagan and Sgurr Mhic Coinnich**

The obvious route to the summits is via the Great Stone Chute, a 380m treadmill of rolling blocks which leads upwards between Sgurr Alasdair and Thearlaich. The scree is now only a remnant of its former glory, having been 'run out' in the past five years by reckless climbers descending the whole scree-run in only a few minutes. Going up is, however, much more laborious, sometimes two steps upward and one back. Two thirds of the way the open scree is enclosed in a wide chimney with sheer precipices to left and right.

Right: **Climbers descending the Great Stone Chute**

The clatter of the scree echoes unnervingly in this tunnel, but the climber should take heart as the broad and level summit of the Chute is soon reached. From here are splendid views, both into Coire a Ghrunnda and across Coire Lagan to the Inaccessible Pinnacle, but the wider view is obscured by the twin summits overhead. A short scramble to the right leads to the summit block of Sgurr Alasdair (993m, 3,257ft), the highest summit in the Cuillin.

Centre: **The Head of the Great Stone Chute**

Left: **Sgurr Dearg from the Summit of Alasdair**

The view from here is magnificent; to the north the summits of Sgurr Dearg and Banachdich can be seen with the Torridon peaks in the distance, and the Isles of Rhum, Eigg and Canna to the South.

So far, this route has not actually followed the main ridge. The climber should retrace his steps to the head of the stone chute and descend a short distance on the Ghrunnda side to a point above the Thearlaich-Dubh gap, where, after a 6m scramble over steep rocks, the crest of the Main Ridge is reached.

Climbing northwards, the top of Sgurr Thearlaich (978m, 3,208ft) is attained without difficulty and the level ridge beyond is easily followed with superb views into Coire an Lochain on the Coruisk side. The route dips downwards and there is some difficult scrambling over slabs which are best taken on the right (eastern) side. In slippery conditions, a rope should be used as the section has a considerable exposure. After a descent of 100m over a short distance along the ridge, one arrives at the Bealach Mhic Coinnich.

15
Right: **The Ridge north from Sgurr Thearlaich**

Sgurr Mhic Coinnich rises above this point like the prow of an ocean liner; the direct climb, graded 'Difficult', is usually tackled by Eponymous chimney. Those less inclined to spend hours dangling on the end of a rope should, however, follow Collie's ledge, an 'Easy' but exposed climb which slants up and left across the 300m rock face above Coire Lagan.

16
Opposite: **Sgurr Mhic Coinnich and Collie's Ledge**

The main ridge is reached some distance north of the summit of Sgurr Mhic Coinnich (948m, 3,111ft), which can be 'bagged' by a short scramble southwards.

Opposite: **Climbers on Collie's Ledge and King's Chimney**

Continuing north, the ridge sinks to Bealach Lagan at 820m before rising again towards An Stac. An obstacle above the bealach is turned on the left by descending the scree a little way. A steep scree slope slanting east is followed upwards until the col between the Inaccessible Pinnacle and An Stac is reached. An Stac (954m, 3,130ft) can be 'bagged' after a short detour. The Pinnacle, however, is a more serious proposition and a rope must be carried to get off this peak, the most difficult 'Munro' in Scotland.

18

Left: **The Inaccessible Pinnacle and An Stac**

The south wall is climbed by a slippery groove to the crest where a 60m scramble ensues with sensational exposure on either hand. At the top a 3m high boulder, the Bolster Stone, is perched. The usual way off the Inaccessible Pinnacle (986m, 3,234ft) is by an abseil of 25m down the western end, using a sling threaded through the stones under the Bolster Stone as an anchor. In wet or slippery conditions the pinnacle is best avoided by following the sloping line at its base up the slabs to the somewhat disappointing summit of Sgurr Dearg (978m, 3,209ft), which is totally overshadowed by the Pinnacle.

19
Opposite: **The Inaccessible Pinnacle from Sgurr Dearg**

To finish this section of the Cuillin, the easy west ridge of Dearg is followed down towards Glenbrittle, skirting a few obstacles, with Thearlaich, Alasdair and the Stone Chute in view across the gulf of Coire Lagan.

20
Above: **Sgurr Banachdich and Ghreadaidh from the Inaccessible Pinnacle**

Beyond Sron Dearg (637m, 2,100ft) grass and scree fall steeply towards Loch an Fhir-bhallaich and the path back to Glenbrittle.

The pleasant walking down the grassy hillside gives time for reflection at the end of one of the most exciting mountain traverses on Skye.
Bruce Herrod

21
See page 5: **The West ridge of Sgurr Dearg**

Below right: **Sron Dearg and the Eas Mor Waterfall**

At the top, the Inaccessible Pinnacle can again be seen, towering above the summit ridge of Sgurr Dearg (978m, 3,209ft). The level ridge narrows and, a short distance away from the Pinnacle, a track begins to descend northwards over the edge. This turn-off point can easily be overlooked in mist or hill fog, and a track along the top, which leads ultimately to a sheer cliff beyond, should not be descended by mistake!

23

Centre: **The Inaccessible Pinnacle from Sgurr Dearg**

The correct route having been taken, a steep track with a drop of nearly 200m leads to the Bealach Coire na Banachdich, this being the lowest point between Dearg and the tops of Sgurr na Banachdich. This bealach can be used to cross the Main Ridge to reach Loch Coruisk and marks the easiest route from Glenbrittle to the loch basin.

24

Far right: **Sgurr Dearg and the Bealach na Banachdich**

The route now rises towards the first of the (unnamed) tops of Banachdich. This forms a grand piece of ridge walking. The notches between the tops require scrambling which can be avoided by a track which runs parallel to the Ridge on the Glenbrittle side.

Section 3 — Sgurr Dearg to Sgurr Ghreadaidh and An Dorus

This section of the Main Ridge traverses four Munros, the traverse across the summit of Sgurr a' Ghreadaidh being one of the longest and certainly the narrowest in the Cuillin.

The climb begins with the ascent of Sgurr Dearg from Glenbrittle. The track across the peat is followed alongside the Allt Coire na Banachdich which flows through a steep sided gorge with the delightful Eas Mor waterfall at its head. From here, the path turns toward Coire Lagan. After fording two streams, the path is abandoned and a direct bee line is made for the Dearg ridge up the cone-like slope of grass and scree which leads to a wide gully. At the top of this, an easier path is followed to the rocks below the subsidiary top of Sron Dearg. A scramble over rocks and around weathered volcanic dykes follows until the crest of the ridge is underfoot.

25

Opposite: **Ascending the Ridge to Banachdich**

There are wonderful views on either side but especially on the right where the crags encircling the basin are mirrored in Loch Coruisk. At the third top, the main peak Sgurr na Banachdich (965m, 3,166ft) is reached where a tiny cairn marks the true summit. From here, the whole of the Main Ridge back to Sgurr Dubh can be viewed.

26

Above: **Loch Coruisk from a notch in the Ridge**

It is, however, best not to dally too long at this delightful spot since the more serious traverse of Thormaid and Ghreadaidh is still to come. The summit of Banachdich is first descended to a broad shelf which forms the junction of three routes: the west ridge to Sgurr nan Gobhar, the northwest ridge to An Diallaid and the north ridge which leads to Bealach Thormaid and the continuation of the Main Ridge. The first two of these routes can provide splendid descents back to Glenbrittle, the Gobhar route being along a spectacular 'Striding edge' similar to Helvellyn in the Lake District. The second, the An Diallaid route, offers the easiest descent back to Glenbrittle if time or bad weather dictates that the full traverse should be curtailed, since the Ghreadaidh section is rather tricky and should never be attempted in mist.

27

Right: **View south from the Summit of Banachdich**

To continue the main ridge traverse, the path from Banachdich summit is followed down to a steep section which turns off to the right. The narrow Bealach Thormaid is reached with sheer drops on either side, but the steeply sloping rock face ahead holds the attention. Although this appears difficult and continuously steep, plenty of good hand and foot holds are to be found. Upward progress is rapid until, after a surprisingly short period of time, you step on to the roof of 'Norman's Peak', Sgurr Thormaid (927m, 3,040ft).

There can be little time for reflection, owing to the exposure on this tiny summit, before descending the smooth sloping slabs on the far side which are very reminiscent of a tiled roof. In the dip which follows, the 'Three Teeth' can be seen. These three small pinnacles sit astride the ridge and can provide some fine scrambling, but are easily avoided by following a wide ledge at their base.

A scramble follows over crumbly, crystalline rocks which rise towards the ensuing summit. The ridge narrows frighteningly, with huge drops on either side, and must be crossed and recrossed several times. The exposure here can be quite unnerving.

Eventually, progress must be made along the razor-like edge with the feet shuffling crab-like along footholds below the undercut crest. In places, the hands must find a grip on the rocks on the other side of the ridge for support!

A 'South Top' at 970m is passed before the true summit of Sgurr a' Ghreadaidh (973m, 3,192ft) is reached. This must rank as the longest, narrowest and, in the Author's opinion, the most sensational summit in Britain, photography on the ridge being out of the question!

28

Below right: **The Knife Edge Summit of Ghreadaidh**

After quitting the summit, the ridge is recrossed to the Coruisk side and a wider sloping path leads down over slabs and around an overhanging rock shoulder known as 'The Wart'. Here, the full length of Loch Coruisk can be viewed lying far below.

Further along, a deep gash in the ridge, the Eag Dubh, must be skirted, in the depths of which the boulders of Coire a Ghreadaidh can be seen over 300m below.

29

Opposite: **Sgurr Ghreadaidh and the Eag Dubh from the corrie**

Finally, one arrives at the pass of An Dorus, 'The Door'. This metre-wide gully comes up from the corrie below to form a perfectly pointed crest and a 5m high rock step must be descended in order to reach it from the track along the ridge. After a few tricky moves, swinging out and down on to this crest, one leaves the ridge and descends left towards Coire a' Ghreadaidh. In mist or bad weather, take care not to descend to the right as this side consists of slabs and steep scree with a hidden 250m precipice.

30
Opposite: **The descent from 'The Wart' to An Dorus**

31
Above: **An Dorus and Sgurr Ghreadaidh with Sgurr Eadar da Choire**

On the Coire a' Ghreadaidh side, the steep scree gully widens out and the slope becomes more bouldery before one arrives in the upper corrie.

Here, a profusion of ice-cold springs are found which gush out of clefts in the rock to form the Allt coire a' Ghreadaidh stream.

Opposite: **Thormaid and Banachdich seen from the Corrie**

This stream tumbles through a succession of delightful ravines containing waterfalls and beautiful blue basins known as the 'Fairy Pools'. The path by the stream should be followed down towards the Glenbrittle Youth Hostel and the road. On a hot day, the traditional end to a fine traverse in superlative mountain scenery is to, at the very least, remove one's boots and socks and bathe tired feet in the magical waters before the final tramp back to the starting point in Glenbrittle.

33
Left: **The 'Fairy Pools' in Coire a'Ghreadaidh**

Section 4 — Sgurr a' Mhadaidh to Bruach na Frithe

This section of the ridge boasts some difficult rock climbing between stretches of easy scrambling or even walking. The major obstacles to be overcome are: the eastern three tops of a' Mhadaidh, the three tops of Bidean Druim nan Ramh and the gap in the ridge just beyond An Caisteal. The whole distance is about 16km (10 miles), of which a large proportion is the return back through the enormous bowl of Coire na Creiche to Glenbrittle.

The best starting point is at the road bridge across the river Brittle. The grassy slope at the foot of Sgurr Thuilm is climbed directly — this is slow going as there is almost 400m of climbing before the gradient eases and Coire a' Ghreadaidh is reached. The panorama from here discloses the peaks of Ghreadaidh, Thormaid and Banachdich on the Main Ridge.

36

Right:
The Highest Summit of Sgurr a'Mhadaidh

At this point, the Main Ridge makes an important turn east, and smooth sloping slabs lead down and round a pinnacle before the next (or third) top of Mhadaidh is attained. The views from the slabs into Coire a' Mhadaidh and to Loch Coruisk are stunning and the feeling of exposure here is very real — this is not a place for those afraid of heights!

It is worthwhile making a detour just before the gap in the ridge to see the impressive northwest spur of the ridge which leads to the conical peak of Sgurr Thuilm. This ridge can provide some exciting scrambling down to a bealach which consists of a narrow wall of blocks. From this point an easy walk leads up to the summit of Sgurr Thuilm from whose viewpoint the whole of the Western part of Skye and the Outer Hebrides beyond can be seen.

37

Opposite: **The West Ridge from Mhadaidh to Thuilm**

To return to the Main Ridge, the stretch from the third top of Mhadaidh across to the Bealach na Glaic Moire traverses the remaining two tops of Mhadaidh. This is strictly rock climbing, with three near vertical pitches of 15m to be surmounted between the first and third tops before an easier scramble of 150m leads down to the bealach.

38

Right: **Loch Coruisk from the Slabs on Mhadaidh**

The continuation of the ridge at this point heads for the triple summits of Bidean Druim nam Ramh (869m, 2,850ft). These cannot be easily traversed and are best avoided by following a broad scree shelf which runs beneath the northern face of the mountain. However, for those who cannot resist a challenge, the Western top (847m, 27,79ft) can be reached from the bealach by an energetic scramble and consists of a massive block of rock perched on the slabs.

39

Opposite: **The Central Peak of Bidean from the North Top**

The Central (and highest) peak (869m, 2,850ft) can be reached from here by an awkward descent to a chockstone known as the 'Bridge Rock'. This is crossed and followed by a climb over slabs to a short chimney before the level, mossy summit platform is attained. The North top (852m, 2,794ft) can be seen across the Gap, a frightening cleft which divides it from the central peak. The Gap is turned with some difficulty over slabs and down a slight overhang. The top is eventually reached by traversing a ledge and climbing directly to the summit, a level platform with rocky seats from which to admire the view and to allow one's nerves to calm down after the climb.

40

Opposite: **Blaven from the Peak of Bidean Druim nam Ramh**

The descent follows the Main Ridge along slabs down to a bealach (760m) at the head of the Coire a Tairneilear. The lateral ridge, which terminates in the minor peak of Sgurr an Fheadain, can be seen to advantage from this point.

41

Left: **Sgurr an Fheadain from the Summit of Bidean**

Continuing along the Main Ridge, a rock step is first encountered, then several 30m deep notches in the ridge must be passed by a courageous stride. Following on, scrambling again, one arrives at the top of An Caisteal (830m, 2,724ft). Direct progress along the Main Ridge from here is barred by a sheer, almost overhanging, drop down to a col which crosses the ridge. Descending the rocks to the right (east) then crossing to the left (Tairneilear side), brings one to a drop of six to 10m which terminates on the crest of the col. This descent is particularly difficult when the rocks are wet. An easier route down from the top is to follow one of the steep gullies which commences about 10m below and to the left of the summit. After a drop of around 30m this gully joins the scree slope descending from the col which can then be reached after an easy climb.

42
Right: **An Caisteal from Coire Tairneilear**

From the col, the rocks forming the continuation of the Main Ridge are easily climbed and, following the crest of the ridge, one quickly arrives at Sgurr na Bhairnich (861m, 2,826ft). This is a relatively featureless summit, consisting of slabs which overhang on the eastern side, but affords fine views down into Lota Corrie and the southeast ridge of Sgurr nan Gillean beyond. From this viewpoint the ridge can be seen twisting northward towards Bruach na Frithe, the next objective.

43
Below right: **Sgurr na Bhairnich and Bruach na Frithe**

After a short scrambling descent from the summit, the broad ridge is now followed northwards by an easy walk at a gentle incline. As one climbs the curving ridge, the rearward view gradually unfolds as height is gained. The twists in the ridge from An Caisteal and across to Sgurr a' Mhadaidh can be seen and beyond are Sgurr Banachdich, Alasdair and nan Eag. With a further short scramble, the summit of Bruach na Frithe (958m, 3,143ft) is attained. This famed viewpoint is the only summit on the Main Ridge to sport an Ordnance Survey triangulation pillar, this being made from cylindrically cast concrete, erected in the centre of a dry stone walled shelter. The view from here extends southward right across the Cuillin.

44
Opposite: **The Twists in the Ridge from Bruach na Frithe**

From the summit of Bruach na Frithe the Main Ridge once again twists eastwards. A broad, well beaten path leads down past Sgurr a Fionn Choire to the Bealach nan Lice and an easy descent into Fionn Choire.
A more exhilarating descent may be made along the crest of the north west ridge, which provides some interesting scrambling down to the grass of the corrie, just above the wide Bealach a Mhaim.

45
Right: **Bruach na Frithe from the Bealach nan Lice**

The five-mile long walk back to Glenbrittle commences with a descent into the wide basin of Coire na Creiche, following the path from the Bealach a Mhaim. Almost the whole of the Main Ridge traverse of this Section can be viewed from the floor of the corrie, and the easy walking gives time for reflection over the difficulties encountered and overcome.

46
Opposite: **The Cuillin Ridge from the Coire na Creiche**

Right: **Sgurr nan Gillean and Sgurr a' Bhasteir**

Numerous waterfalls are passed as the path rises to the 300m contour, where a sketchy track is followed south after crossing the burn. This rises into Fionn Choire at first over grass and then more steeply over boulders and scree.

The final part of the ascent is up a steep yellowish coloured track which levels out suddenly at the Bealach nan Lice, marked with a large cairn and having several routes radiating from it. A track from here runs north along the top of the subsidiary ridge to Sgurr a' Bhasteir, which is often mistaken for Bruach na Frithe when seen from the road at Sligachan.

From the bealach, Harta Corrie can be seen far below on the south side of the ridge.

48

Opposite: **Sgurr a' Bhasteir and Sligachan from Bealach nan Lice**

Sgurr a Fionn Choire (935m, 3,068ft) can be reached by turning right (west) along the path towards Bruach na Frithe and, after reaching a small col at 905m (2,968ft), a short scramble eastwards leads to the summit of the peak. The ridge cannot easily be continued from here due to huge overhangs above the Bealach nan Lice, and the safest way to continue is to retrace one's steps back to the bealach.

Section 5 — Sgurr a' Fionn Choire to Sgurr nan Gillean and h-Uamha

This, the final section of the Main Ridge of the Cuillin, runs east-west to the major peak, Sgurr nan Gillean, and then turns south to the terminus of the horseshoe, the miniature peak Sgurr na h-Uamha. The strict traverse across the summits is a major mountaineering exercise for a roped party, although all of the tops, with the exception of the Basteir Tooth, can be reached by a detour.

The start and finish for this route is the car park at the Sligachan Hotel. The view of Sgurr nan Gillean from this point is splendid, although the northern pinnacles cannot be seen from this direction. Across the road a track leads through the peat bogs towards the mountains, then follows the left bank of the Allt Dearg Mor stream towards the wide Bealach a Mhaim.

49

Right: **Sgurr a' Fionn Choire, Am Basteir and Sgurr nan Gillean**

From the cairn, a path descends east at the foot of Am Basteir, 'The Executioner', and the Basteir Tooth which hangs overhead like a 60m high axe blade. Both routes to the top of this formidable obstacle consist of long 'Severe' rock climbs and should be left strictly alone by all but experienced climbing parties. After a traversing descent of about 60m along the foot of Am Basteir, a rising track on the scree is soon encountered, which brings one to the Main Ridge once more at a point mid-way between Am Basteir and Sgurr nan Gillean. This is the Bealach a Basteir, a difficult pass across the ridge into Lota and Harta Corries. To reach the top of Am Basteir, turn East along the ridge and, after a short walk, rocks must be surmounted which are easier on the right (north) side. The top of Am Basteir (935m, 3,069ft) gives a strong impression of 'hanging in mid air' since there are 180m sheer drops on three sides. Looking down the western precipice, only the tip of the Tooth can be seen.

Left: **Am Basteir and the Tooth**

Again retracing one's steps to the Bealach, there are impressive views down into the Coire a Basteir and the Basteir Gorge. The Pinnacle ridge of Gillean can be seen from here too; five separate rocky spires of cathedral proportions and increasing heights, culminating in the peak of Sgurr nan Gillean itself, the next objective on this traverse. From the Bealach, rock spurs and gullies prevent the west ridge of Gillean from being reached directly. A level traverse of about 40m to the left, however, reveals Nicholson's chimney; a 25m high gully which, in dry conditions, is rather easier to climb than it looks.

Opposite: **The Pinnacles of Sgurr nan Gillean and the Basteir Gorge**

At the top there are numerous large unstable blocks on the ridge, one in particular known as the 'Gendarme' or policeman, a large loose block sitting astride the crest. A difficult step across a gap, or rather a long stride, is required, giving an anxious moment without the security of a rope belay. This brings one to rather more secure footing. The remainder of the west ridge is then ascended by scrambling around various loose blocks until, with a final 'heave', the summit table is attained.

52

Left: **Climbers about to Descend Nicholson's Chimney**

This, the summit of Sgurr nan Gillean (965m, 3,167ft) is one of the finest in the Cuillins, the supporting ridges on the south and east sides being quite invisible from the top. The top consists of a level block of around four metres in length, cracked at the middle, with a large cairn at the southern end. The view back down the west ridge is particularly impressive, daylight being clearly visible under some of the blocks.

The views to the north and east and especially along the full length of Glen Sligachan to Blaven are particularly fine. The rounded red Cuillin hills to the east of the glen from Glamaig to Marsco are very distinctive.

53

Right: **The West Ridge to Am Basteir from the Summit of nan Gillean**

Sgurr nan Gillean is often considered to form the terminus of the Main Ridge of the Cuillin. However, a continuation of the ridge runs southeast from nan Gillean for almost a mile across the minor tops of Sgurr Beag and Sgurr na h-Uamha before descending into the depths of Harta Corrie.

54

Opposite: **Descending the SE ridge of nan Gillean**

The descent from nan Gillean follows the southeast ridge which is normally the most common route of ascent — the 'Tourist Route'. This title, however, belies the fact that it is, in the upper parts, a difficult and exposed scramble.

The summit platform is first descended by stepping across a notch and then down some steep smooth slabs, the crest of the ridge being alarmingly narrow at this point.

Right: **Sgurr nan Gillean in winter**

Further down, some awkward corners must be descended before the going becomes easier. The two summits of Sgurr Beag and na h-Uamha can now be seen ahead.

At an altitude of approximately 730m, one arrives at a wide plateau which forms the normal route of descent to Sligachan. Sgurr Beag (765m, 2,511ft) can be reached by continuing along the ridge and then east to a broad, crescent shaped summit, offering panoramic views of Gillean and Glen Sligachan.

The final stretch of the ridge leads due south from Sgurr Beag to a grassy bealach, the Bealach a Ghlas Coire. From here the route to the top of the final peak looks innocuous enough. However, after crossing a connecting ridge the difficulties lying ahead can be seen and an exciting straight rock climb is needed to attain this final summit, Sgurr na h-Uamha (736m, 2,416ft) a worthy terminus to the Cuillin horseshoe of peaks.

The top is flat and spacious with crags on all three sides, and there are impressive views of the Main Ridge to Bidean Druim nan Ramh across the depths of Harta Corrie. There is only one feasible route of descent — the same as that of the ascent.

56

Above left: **Sgurr na h-Uamha**

On regaining the bealach, a descent can be made down the screes into An Glas choire and thence into Glen Sligachan. However, it is easier and quicker to reclimb the ridge to a point just beyond Sgurr Beag where the 'Tourist Route' can be joined.

The path back to Sligachan is nowadays showing signs of the numerous hordes of visitors attempting the ascent of nan Gillean, with parallel cairned tracks much in evidence across the scree above Coire Riabhach. The huge bulk of Blaven — a worthy climb for another day — can be seen across the Glen from the cluster of small tarns in Coire Riabhach.

57

Left: **Coire Riabhach and Blaven on the return from nan Gillean**

The footbridge across the Allt Dearg Beag torrent is soon reached and then a final hike takes one across the spongy peat which leads to the doors of the Sligachan Hotel.

After completing the traverse of the whole of the Main Cuillin ridge, the only fitting tribute is to toast the Hills with a large dram of Talisker in one of the hotel bars!

58

See page 3

The Misty Isle hides the secrets of the Cuillins

Right: **Sgurr nan Gillean from Glen Sligachan**

After an initial gradient, the path levels off and heads south down the glen, fording a few minor streams on the way. After the first mile, the gaps between the pinnacles of Sgurr nan Gillean become apparent and climbers can sometimes be spotted on the southeast ridge or 'Tourist Route' of the mountain. At a distance of 6km (four miles) from Sligachan, the Lochan Dubha — two small tarns — is passed. In the distance beyond, the expanse of Harta Corrie opens out and the western peaks of the Cuillin including the Inaccessible Pinnacle can be viewed.

Opposite: **Harta Corrie and the Peaks of the Main Ridge**

At this point the path forks, the left hand branch crossing a stream and heading down the valley towards the Loch an Athain and the huge northwest face of Blaven.

Taking the right fork, however, a few peaty streams must be forded before the path begins to rise towards the pass over the Druim Hain ridge. A gentle top is crossed at a height of about 300m (1,000ft). The panoramic view from this small plateau covers the whole of the main ridge of the Cuillin, on a clear day all of the major peaks from Gars Bheinn to Sgurr nan Gillean being in view.

Section 6 — Sligachan to Loch Coruisk

Every climber has an 'off day' when a change from scrambling across the peaks is needed. However, fine days spent on Skye out of sight of the Cuillin are usually repented at leisure, and so the walk down Glen Sligachan to Loch Coruisk is a welcome diversion. Most of the Cuillin peaks can be seen from a new viewpoint on the way and although the distance is long (12km or 7.5 miles each way), the walking is very easy and the gradient moderate.

The walk commences at the Sligachan hotel and, after crossing the old stone bridge across the Sligachan river, the path signposted 'To Loch Coruisk' is taken. Since this signpost does not quote the distance, many tourists are passed during the first half mile searching for the loch!

61

Opposite: **Loch an Athain and Blaven from the Glen**

The path leads down over the other side of the pass towards Loch Scavaig and the sea. Loch Coruisk cannot yet be seen at this point, being hidden behind the ridge of Druim nam Ramh. A small lochan, Loch a Riabhaich, is passed on the descent and shortly afterwards Loch Coruisk comes into view, nestling in the huge rock basin of Coir' Uisg, with the massive East face of Sgurr a Ghreadaidh at its northwestern extremity.

The path is followed down to the loch shore — this is fresh water and, on a hot day, water bottles can be filled. The scene here is splendidly tranquil, few tourists finding their way to this spot unless ferried-in by boat from Elgol.

62

Above left: **Coir' Uisg and Loch Coruisk**

Further on, at the southern end of the loch, the short river Scavaig flows for only 300m to the sea — almost the shortest river in Scotland. This can be crossed in dry weather by a series of stepping stones, but in times of spate the river widens and the smooth slabs can be extremely dangerous.

63

Below left: **Loch Scavaig from the river.**

At this end of the Coir' Uisg basin, the rocks are in the form of rounded masses of Gabbro, shaped by ancient glaciers and covered with needle sharp crystals, exposed by the weathering of the rock surface.

64
Right: **Loch Coruisk from Sgurr na Stri**

The return is best made by the path back to Sligachan. An alternative but exhausting return can be taken in superb scenery by walking around the head of the loch and following a track which heads north up to the Bealach na Glaic Moire. This crosses the Main Ridge between Sgurr a Mhadaidh and Bidean Druim nam Ramh and descends into Coire na Creiche. Owing to the difficult terrain of the ridge and the fact that the Bealach a Mhaim must be crossed to reach Sligachan, this return route can only be recommended to Supermen who have traversed this section of the Main Ridge before!

65
See page 1
Ghreadaidh, Mhadaidh and Bidean seen from Loch Coruisk

Section 7 — The Blaven — Clach Glas Traverse

Although separated from the main area of the Cuillin by the huge rift of Glen Sligachan, the chain of peaks of Bla Bheinn (Blaven), Clach Glas and Sgurr nan Each have a great deal in common with the peaks of the Main Cuillin Ridge. This traverse of the summits is also highly rated as one of the finest in Scotland. The climb is usually taken from north to south, the difficulties on Clach Glas being easier to surmount from this direction.

The route commences on the Torrin to Elgol road near the head of Loch Slapin. A boggy path is followed by the side of the Allt na Dunaiche burn into Coire a Caise. This climbs steadily until, at an altitude of around 200m (650ft) a sketchy track is taken northwards which leads to the grassy east ridge of Sgurr nan Each. This is followed to the East top of the mountain and a gradual climb leads from here to the main top (Sgurr nan Each, 716m, 2,350ft).

66
Left: **Blaven from Coire Uaigneich**

From the summit a descent, still in a westerly direction, leads to the Bealach Buttress which forms the head of Coire a Caise. After crossing the top of this buttress, the head of the Arch gully is seen descending into the depths of the Coire Dubh. The route now turns due south through 90 degrees and the ascent of Clach Glas begins. This is a straight scramble upward, past a series of pinnacles and up a stone filled gully. Finally, broken rocks are climbed to the summit of Clach Glas (787m, 2,582ft). The descent from this point begins with 'The Imposter', so called by the early climbers because passing this obstacle is easier than it seems at first sight.

The sloping roof of the summit is descended to an overhang with a drop on to a level ridge. A steep awkward gully follows, and then you step onto an unexpectedly grassy hollow known as 'The Putting Green', actually the Blaven-Clach Glas bealach. A huge scree run falls from here down to Coire Dubh and Glen Sligachan.

67
Right: **Clach Glas and 'The Putting Green' from Blaven**

Continuing southwest towards Blaven, the 'Putting Green' gives way to a steep 5m high wall which should be climbed, leading to a scree amphitheatre with the 'Half Crown Pinnacle' towering above. The scree beyond this is ascended to a platform where a stony chimney leads to a scree gully which exits on to the east ridge.

A simple albeit steep walk follows to the summit of Blaven (928m, 3,044ft) which is marked with a large cairn and a Triangulation column. The views from here are tremendous, notably along Glen Sligachan with the Black Cuillin to the left and the Red Cuillin to the right. The pinnacle ridge of Sgurr nan Gillean is particularly prominent from this viewpoint.

68
Opposite: **Glen Sligachan from the Summit of Blaven**

The South Top of Blaven (924m), only 4m lower than the true summit, is reached by a 15m descent to a bealach, followed by a short scramble up a chimney which emerges to the north of the summit platform.

The mountain may be descended by a track heading eastwards which zig-zags down to a bealach above Fionna choire at 620m. A descent northeast then leads to a path which descends into Coire Uaigneich, skirting the screes which fall from the vast buttresses of Blaven and Clach Glas. The path beyond crosses the burn and continues back to the road.

69
Opposite: **Blaven in Winter**

A more interesting descent may be made from the summit by following the ridge south to Camasunary on the shore of Loch Scavaig. From the South Summit, the wide crest of the ridge is descended, bypassing the heads of gullies which emerge from the northeast face, a total of four 'False Summits' being passed on the way down. All is pleasant walking on grass covered slabs with easy rock steps between.

When a level grassy plateau is reached at a height of 350m, a stony gully to the left is descended and the grass hillside is crossed to the Abhainn nan Leac burn. Following the burn past two waterfalls, the main Sligachan to Camasunary path is soon joined.

A long walk back over the shoulder of the Beinn Leacach leads to the Elgol road. The long trek back to the starting point is eased by fine views across the deep blue of Loch Slapin to the Sleat peninsular.

70
Above: **The twin summits of Blaven from Torrin**

Postscript

The Cuillins in winter! In a covering of ice and snow, the mountains are transformed into virgin Alpine peaks. Pinnacles and gullies stand out against the bare rock faces, and the rocky corries are smothered into white basins.

I spent the Christmas of 1993 at Sconser near Sligachan and climbed high into the mountains across the deep powdery snow. The amount of snow was unusual for Skye, and the mountains were a fairyland of snow gullies, cornices, icicles and ice encrusted rock. I ventured into Coire a'Bhasteir and up towards the SE ridge of Sgurr nan Gillean and the solitude was intense. For days, mine were the only footsteps to be seen and followed. Each time, thigh-deep snow eventually forced my cautious retreat without reaching the Main Ridge, but the superb scenery made up for any disappointment over not reaching the summits. Just to be there was reward enough!

71
Below: **The Cuillins in winter**

Glossary of Gaelic Words and Pronunciation

Word	Pronunciation	Translation
abhainn	-avan	River
all't	-alt	Burn, stream
allt	-alt	Burn, stream
athain	-a-theyn	(of the) River
banachdich	-bana'dich	(Possibly) Pockmarked
basteir	-basitter	Executioner
beag	-beg	Small, little
bealach	-bay-allach	Pass
beinn	-ben	Mountain
bhairnich	-vair-nich	Limpet
bhallaich	-val-aych	Speckled
bhasteir	-basitter	Executioner
bheinn	-ven	Mountain
bhig	-vick	Little
bidean	-bidjin	Peak
bla-bheinn	-bla-ven	Blue mountain
blaven	-bla-ven	Blue mountain
bruach	-brew-ach	Brae
caise	-careesa	Rushing
caisteal	-cas-tel	Castle
camas Fhionnairigh	-camas-sionair	Fair Shieling
choire	-horry	Kettle, high valley
chruidh	-croo-ee	Cattle
ciche	-kee-sher	Breast
cioch	-hee-och	Breast
clach	-klach	Stones
coir	-korr	Kettle, high valley
coire-Uisg	-korr-uisk	Cauldron of the waters
coruisk	-korr-uisk	" "
creiche	-hree-sher	Spoils or Booty
cuillin	-coolin	(Possibly) Holly
dearg	-jerrack	Red
diallaid	-jee-lich	Saddle
dorus	-dorrush	Door
druim	-drum	Ridge
dubh	-doo	Black
dubha	-doo-ah	"
dunaiche	-doo-naich	Misfortune
each	-ay-ach	Horse
eadar	-ay-dar	Between
eag	-eck	Chasm or Cliff
eas	-eyas	Waterfall
fheadain	-ait-yan	Chanters or Pipes

Word	Pronunciation	Translation
fhir	-eer	Folk, Men
fionn	-fee-on	Fair
fionna	-fee-onna	"
frithe	-free	Forest
garbh	-garra	Rough
ghlas	-glas	Grey
ghreadaidh	-hree-tay	Storms
ghrunnda	-hroonda	Bare, gloomy
gillean	-Gill-ean	Young Men
glaic	-gleyk	Gorge, defile
glamaig	-glam-eyk	Greedy Woman
glas	-glas	Grey
gobhar	-go-ar	Goat
hain	-hine	Hinds
harta	-har-ta	Hart
leac	-lay-ak	Rock Platform
leacach	-lay-acht	Flat Rocks
lochain	-loch-an	Little loch
lochan	-loch-an	" "
lota	-low-ta	Lofty
marsco	-mars-ko	Seagull Rock
mhadaidh	-vattee, vardy	Fox
mhaim	-vaim or vyme	Moor
mhic coinnich	-vick hoe-innich	MacKenzie
ramh	-raahv	Oars
riabhach	-reea-vach	Brindled, Russet
riabhaich	-reea-vaych	" "
scavaig	-ska-vayg	Gloomy
sgumain	-skooman	Stack
sgurr	-skoor	Peak
slapin	-sla-pin	Muddy, Sluggish
sleat	-slate	Mountain Slopes
sligachan	-sliga-han	Shelly place
soay	-soy	Swine, (Isle of)
sron	-shron	Hump or shoulder
stac	-stack	Stack
stri	-stree	Winds or Strife
tairneilear	-tar-na-lear	Thunderer
thearlaich	-chair'lich	Charles
thormaid	-horro'mid	Norman
thuilm	-hoolim	Tulm (Gaelic hero)
uaigneich	-oo-aig-nich	Hidden or Solitude
uamha	-oo-ah-va	Cave
uisg	-oo-isk	Water — as in Whisky